AMAZING
DINOSAURS

Sandy Creek
NEW YORK

Sandy Creek
NEW YORK

An Imprint of Sterling Publishing
387 Park Avenue South
New York, NY 10016

SANDY CREEK and the distinctive Sandy Creek logo
are registered trademarks of Barnes & Noble, Inc.

© 2012 by Amber Books Ltd

This 2012 edition is published by Sandy Creek.

Editorial and design by
Amber Books Ltd
74–77 White Lion Street
London N1 9PF
United Kingdom

Contributing Authors: David Alderton, Susan Barraclough, Per Christiansen, Kieron Connolly,
Paula Hammond, Tom Jackson, Claudia Martin, Carl Mehling, Veronica Ross, Sarah Uttridge
Consulting Editor: Per Christiansen
Series Editor: Sarah Uttridge
Editorial Assistant: Kieron Connolly
Designer: Andrew Easton
Picture Research: Terry Forshaw

ISBN 978-1-4351-4273-2

For information about custom editions, special sales, and premium and corporate purchases, please contact
Sterling Special Sales at 800-805-5489 or specialsales@sterlingpublishing.com.

Manufactured in China

Lot #:
2 4 6 8 10 9 7 5 3 1
09/12

Contents

Introduction

Dinosaurs lived on Earth millions of years before we did. Even though no human being has ever seen a dinosaur, we still know a lot about them. Many dinosaur bones, teeth, or fossils have been found all over the world. Scientists have worked out what the dinosaurs looked like, how they moved and what—or who—they ate. Dinosaur means "very terrible lizard."

Coelurosauravus

Coelurosauravus was not a dinosaur itself. However, it was an ancestor of later reptiles, including dinosaurs. It probably lived in forests and ate big insects. It may also have hunted and rested in small flocks, like some modern birds. Its wings were built like paper fans and allowed it to glide from tree to tree.

WHERE DID THEY LIVE?

Fossils have been found in Germany, England, and Madagascar.

Europe

Africa

Madagascar

Fingers

Flexible fingers with claws helped it to grab and hold on to high perches.

Teeth

Rows of sharp teeth crunched up big, juicy insects.

DID YOU KNOW?

The skull was light and like a lizard's skull. It had a pointed snout and a jaw filled with sharp teeth.

Coelurosauravus had retractable wings made from skin that grew on each side of its body. They were supported by rodlike bones. These bones were not attached to its ribcage.

The small head had a lightweight skull. This helped *Coelurosauravus* stay in the air for as long as possible.

FACTS

- One of the earliest gliding reptiles known.

- Its wing design was unique and hasn't been seen on any reptile since *Coelurosauravus* died out.

- Lived during the Permian period.

SIZE

Dimetrodon

This fearsome beast had a huge arching sail on its back and a vicious set of teeth. *Dimetrodon* stalked the Earth more than 260 million years ago. It was probably the top predator on land at that time. It killed its prey with bites from its stabbing fangs and sliced off flesh with its sharp teeth. The sail on its back may have warmed the reptile up after a cold night.

WHERE DID THEY LIVE?

Found in Permian deposits in the USA and Europe.

North America

Europe

Jaws

These were strong and full of lethal teeth for killing and tearing apart prey.

Sail

Many people think that the sail helped to regulate body temperature.

FACTS

SIZE

- Some people think that the sail was used like an actual sail on a boat, helping it to swim.

- This is not an actual dinosaur. It lived 40 million years before the dinosaurs and is a relative of mammals.

DID YOU KNOW?

Dimetrodon walked more upright than most other reptiles. This made it a faster-moving predator.

It was a cold-blooded animal. Cold-blooded animals need much less energy than warm-blooded animals. This means they also need less food. If they need less food, more can survive on the same piece of land. Therefore, it's possible that there were a great many *Dimetrodon* in the world.

Coelophysis

Coelophysis probably lived in herds, prowling the land in large numbers. Hunting together, they may have been able to attack larger prey than they could on their own. It may also have eaten its own young. It had a streamlined shape, a lightweight skeleton, and long muscular legs. *Coelophysis* was a very good runner. It could twist and turn at top speed.

WHERE DID THEY LIVE?

Found in Arizona and New Mexico, in the USA

USA

Arizona
● ●
New Mexico

Teeth

Coelophysis had more than 100 daggerlike teeth for ripping into flesh.

Eyes

Forward-facing eyes and keen nostrils helped the beast find its next meal.

FACTS

- This is one of the earliest known dinosaurs to roam the Earth.

- A flexible neck helped it to grab prey.

- Lived during the Mid-Triassic period.

SIZE

DID YOU KNOW?

- U.S. fossil hunter Edward Drinker Cope named *Coelophysis* in 1889.

- Not all adult *Coelophysis* fossil remains are the same. There are two forms of the dinosaur, and one is larger than the other. Experts think the larger ones are males and the smaller ones are females, but not everyone agrees.

- *Coelophysis* had long, flexible arms with long fingers and large, sharp claws. These were good for catching small, fast prey such as lizards.

Cynognathus

This fierce predator looked like a cross between a wolf and a lizard. *Cynognathus* was a top predator in its environment. It hunted in a pack so it could attack larger animals. One of its possible prey animals was *Kannemeyeria*. This was a herbivore twice its length. A secondary palate in its mouth meant that it could breathe and swallow at the same time.

WHERE DID THEY LIVE?

In Argentina, the Karoo Basin of South Africa, China, and Antarctica.

Asia

South Africa

Argentina

Antarctica

Legs

Cynognathus ran quickly on short, muscular legs. Its backbone moved more from side to side so it ran with a waddle.

FACTS

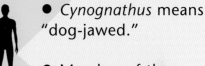

- Huge and powerful jaws opened wide.
- *Cynognathus* means "dog-jawed."
- Member of the cynodont family from the Triassic period.

Teeth

Sharp canine teeth and nipping incisor teeth pierced blood vessels and ripped through flesh.

DID YOU KNOW?

Cynognathus was stockily built. It had a massive head that made up one-third of its total length.

This reptilelike mammal has a lot in common with modern mammals: its legs were positioned under its body, it seems to have had warm blood, it may have given birth to live young rather than eggs, and it had whiskers.

Its body may have been covered in fur to prevent heat loss during cold nights.

Gracilisuchus

Gracilisuchus looks like a dinosaur, but actually it is a relative of crocodiles. Unlike today's crocodiles, it walked on two legs and lived on the land. People thought it was a dinosaur when it was first discovered in the 1970s. It lived among the earliest dinosaurs. It could snatch small fish from water, chase lizards on land, and pluck insects out of the air.

WHERE DID THEY LIVE?

Remains were found in Argentina in the 1970s.

South
America

Argentina

Claws

The front limbs
ended in long
razor-sharp claws.

FACTS

- *Gracilisuchus* means "slender crocodile."

SIZE

- The front limbs were two-thirds the length of the back limbs.

- Lived during the Triassic period.

Jaws

Long well-muscled
jaws held the reptile's
victims in a very
strong grip.

DID YOU KNOW?

The head was very large compared to its slender body. This suggests that it used its jaws to catch prey rather than using its claws.

The teeth were straight and pointed. They were perfect for puncturing the bodies of small reptiles and insects.

Gracilisuchus had big eyes. This suggests that the animal hunted mainly by sight.

Lystrosaurus

Lystrosaurus was a mammal ancestor. It was herbivorous and lived in large groups. It was very common on the dry plains during the Permian and Early Triassic Period. And it is one of the few therapsids (mammal ancestors) to survive from the Permian to the Triassic Period. It was probably eaten by larger predators that were faster-moving.

WHERE DID THEY LIVE?

Across the world, in Antarctica, South Africa, India, Russia, Mongolia, China, and Australia.

Asia

Africa

Australia

Antarctica

DID YOU KNOW?

Lystrosaurus had tusks that would have helped it to dig up plant roots and to scare off predators.

Its jaw moved backward and forward when it was eating, instead of the more common up and down or sideways movements.

Lystrosaurus was about 5–6.6 ft (1.5–2 m) ft long and weighed about 100–200 lbs (50–90 kg).

Legs

Its stumpy feet meant that it was slow-moving.

Beak

The sharp, horny beak was perfect for gathering plants and cutting through tough stems.

FACTS

• *Lystrosaurus* means "shovel lizard."

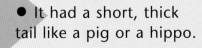

• It had a short, thick tail like a pig or a hippo.

• It had two tusks but no teeth.

SIZE

Scelidosaurus

Scelidosaurus was a slow-moving plant-eater. It was lightly armored as protection from predators. but was a relative of the armored dinosaurs. It is possible it reared up on its hindlegs to reach higher foliage, but its four feet were all the same size. This suggests that it mainly walked on all-fours. It had four toes on each foot.

WHERE DID THEY LIVE?

Discovered in 1861 in layers of limestone and shale in Dorset, England.

England
Dorset

Skin

Embedded in the thick, scaly skin were large, round nodules of bone, which were called scutes.

FACTS

SIZE

- The hind legs were much longer and stronger than the forelimbs.

- *Scelidosaurus* means "limb lizard."

- Lived during the Early Jurassic period.

DID YOU KNOW?

The tail helped to balance the dinosaur as it walked. It may also have supported it when rearing up to reach food.

To protect itself from larger, faster predators, *Scelidosaurus* probably crouched down until its belly was against the ground, leaving only its armored back and sides exposed.

The small, bony beak, and simple leaf-shaped teeth were characteristic of plant-eating dinosaurs.

Beak

The small, horn-covered beak was used to snip off leaves and small twigs.

Dimorphodon

Dimorphodon was one of the earliest pterosaurs, or flying reptiles. It had a huge head, but there were large openings between its skull bones, so its head did not weigh much. It had unusually deep jaws for a pterosaur. It had good vision and a long tail. It was able to fly steadily for a long time but could also make sudden dives to attack prey.

WHERE DID THEY LIVE?

Lyme Regis, England. It is the home of Dinosaurland Fossil Museum.

England
Lyme Regis

Eyes

Large eyes gave *Dimorphodon* excellent vision, like a modern bird of prey.

FACTS

SIZE

- *Dimorphodon* means "two types of teeth."

- It probably laid eggs, although no fossilized ones have been found.

- Lived during the Mid-Jurassic period.

Skin

The thick skin of the wings was reinforced with fibers, like the spokes of an umbrella.

DID YOU KNOW?

At the front of the mouth were long teeth for gripping slippery fish. At the sides were smaller, spiky teeth, probably used for slicing through flesh.

The long, stiff tail counterbalanced the weight of the head. This made it more stable when flying. The diamond-shaped skin-flap probably helped it to steer.

Dimorphodon is often shown as having a puffinlike beak. It used this to snap up small animals.

Megalosaurus

Megalosaurus lived around 170 million years ago. At this time, the landscape was filled with giant trees, which were a mixture of true trees such as conifers, giant ferns, and horsetails. This foliage allowed *Megalosaurus* to hide from its prey before launching an attack. It was able to kill dinosaurs much bigger than itself.

WHERE DID THEY LIVE?

Fossil remains were first discovered in Oxfordshire, England.

England
●
Oxford

FACTS

- *Megalosaurus* means "great lizard."

- *Megalosaurus* walked upright on two legs.

- Lived during the Mid-Jurassic period.

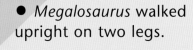

SIZE

Claws

These were long, hooked, and sharp for ripping through tough skin.

Teeth

Sharp, bladelike, and numerous, these were the dinosaur's primary weapons.

DID YOU KNOW?

Megalosaurus was the first dinosaur to be described. It was also one of the first dinosaurs to be given a scientific name. This happened before the word "dinosaur" had even been introduced.

Megalosaurus had a large skull and strong jaw muscles. It had quite small eyes and relied on smell when hunting.

The jaws could move sideways. This meant that *Megalosaurus* could shear off huge mouthfuls, which it then swallowed whole.

Shunosaurus

This long-necked plant-eater had little to fear from its enemies. *Shunosaurus* was armed with a lethal, spiked club on the end of its tail. This could have sliced open an attacker with a single blow. *Shunosaurus* probably traveled in herds, eating horsetails, ferns, and other plants that were around in the Jurassic period. It had to eat a vast amount to fill its large stomach.

WHERE DID THEY LIVE?

China

All specimens are from China's Sichuan Province.

FACTS

• *Shunosaurus* means "lizard from Shu."

• It has a club at the end of the tail. This was only discovered in 1989.

• Lived during the Mid-Jurassic period.

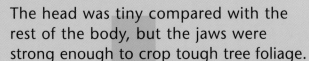

SIZE

Tail

As well as being used as a weapon, the tail counterbalanced the animal's long neck.

Legs

Strong and stout like an elephant's, the legs held the body clear of the ground.

DID YOU KNOW?

The big body held the large stomach and long intestine needed to digest the dinosaur's fibrous vegetable food.

More than 20 complete *Shunosaurus* skeletons have been found and every one of its bones is known. This is very unusual. The number of finds suggests that it was common in the Mid-Jurassic.

The head was tiny compared with the rest of the body, but the jaws were strong enough to crop tough tree foliage.

Allosaurus

Allosaurus was a fearsome killing machine. It was fast, powerful, and able to attack anything it came across. It was the top predator for more than 10 million years. It seized prey with its muscular front limbs, inflicting terrible wounds with its sharp claws. It was a fast runner, but the top half of its body was heavy and it risked serious injury if it fell onto its short front arms.

WHERE DID THEY LIVE?

USA • Portugal •

Mostly the USA, with others found in Portugal, and possibly Tanzania and Australia.

Teeth

Each jaw had 30 or more teeth. New teeth grew to replace ones lost during fights.

Hands

Each hand had three sharp claws that could cut through flesh.

FACTS

- *Allosaurus* means "strange lizard".

- The claws could be up to 6 in (15 cm) long.

- Lived during the Late Jurassic period.

SIZE

DID YOU KNOW?

This dinosaur's top half was very heavy. Without its massive tail to help with balance, it would have fallen over.

Allosaurus had a bony bump above each eye, and a bony ridge from the forehead to the tip of the snout. The purpose of this is not known, but it may have been a mark of rank among the dinosaurs.

The large muscular legs allowed it to sprint at prey. It may have emerged from trees close to water holes where it drank.

Apatosaurus

Apatosaurus was a sauropod. These were enormous, long-necked, long-tailed, plant-eating dinosaurs. This animal needed to eat several hundred pounds of spiky leaves every day and probably munched for most of its waking hours. Fossils show that this giant-sized dinosaur had legs like tree trunks and a massive body that was the size of four or five African elephants.

WHERE DID THEY LIVE?

Many fossils have been found in Wyoming in the USA.

Wyoming
USA

Tail

The tip of the tail would have cracked like a gunshot when the tail was whipped.

FACTS

SIZE

- *Apatosaurus* means "false lizard."

- Teeth like pegs raked foliage and teeth like chisels snipped stems.

- Lived during the Late Jurassic period.

Feet

Huge flat-soled feet spread the heavy load of the dinosaur.

DID YOU KNOW?

Apatosaurus reared up on its hind legs to reach the tops of trees. Its tail pressed against the ground to help with balance.

Othniel Marsh named *Apatosaurus* in 1877 and *Brontosaurus* in 1879. He did not realize that his later discovery was also *Apatosaurus* bones. The name *Brontosaurus* is not used today.

An adult *Apatosaurus* may have had 99 lb (45 kg) of stones in its gizzard (foregut) to grind up the plant food that it ate.

Archaeopteryx

Archaeopteryx is the earliest known bird. It had the teeth, claws, and tail of a killer dinosaur—and the feathers of a bird. It probably lived in open forest, gliding between trees. *Archaeopteryx* was about the size of a pigeon. Its mix of features suggests that it was a halfway stage in the development of birds from reptiles. Its remains hold clues to the evolution of flight in birds.

WHERE DID THEY LIVE?

Southern Germany. The limestone has preserved the impressions of its feathers.

Germany

Europe

Wings

The design of the wing was better suited for gliding than for flapping.

FACTS

SIZE

- *Archaeopteryx* means "ancient wing."

- Its feathers insulated the bird and controlled its body temperature.

- Lived during the Late Jurassic period.

Feet

Three toes pointed forward and one backward. This provided a good perching grip.

DID YOU KNOW?

The jaws were lined with sharp, pointed teeth, like those of other meat-eating dinosaurs.

Debate continues about whether *Archaeopteryx* took off in flight by dropping out of trees or by running along the ground first in search of small animals to eat.

Modern birds have no tail bones, but *Archaeopteryx* had a long, bony tail more like a reptile.

Brachiosaurus

The ground would have shaken as *Brachiosaurus* lumbered through the prehistoric forests. This dinosaur was as heavy as eight fully grown African elephants. Its immense size made it scary for potential enemies. It had a hugely long neck that meant it could reach as high as a three-story building to eat the leaves at the tops of trees. It may also have used its neck as a weapon.

WHERE DID THEY LIVE?

First discovered in western Colorado, USA, and since in southern Europe, north Africa and Tanzania.

North America

Europe

Africa

Neck

The neck made up half of the animal's great height.

FACTS

- *Brachiosaurus* means "arm reptile."

- This was one of the largest dinosaurs of the Jurassic period.

- It was not able to chew.

SIZE

Teeth

The teeth were like peg-shaped chisels. They could nip off fresh shoots at the tops of trees.

DID YOU KNOW?

Brachiosaurus probably needed several hundred pounds of food every day.

Brachiosaurus had a very powerful heart so it could pump blood along its long neck to its brain. The neck would have had muscular blood vessels with many valves to prevent the blood flowing backward.

The skull had many hollows to make it lighter. Lifting a solid skull on such a long neck would have been impossible.

Compsognathus

The size of a small chicken, *Compsognathus* was once the smallest dinosaur known to us. Now we know there were other small and even smaller dinosaurs. It was quick—a lizard would have had to run very fast to escape its jaws. It had powerful hind legs, excellent eyesight, and a birdlike beak. It lived on small islands where there was scrubby vegetation.

WHERE DID THEY LIVE?

Near Nice in southern France. It has also been found in Germany.

Germany

Europe

France

Plumage

Compsognathus was probably covered in fine, downy feathers.

FACTS

SIZE

- *Compsognathus* means "delicate jaw."

- *Compsognathus* is one of the smallest non-avian dinosaurs known.

- Lived during the Late Jurassic period.

Teeth

Small, sharp teeth were ideal for chomping down on lizards, insects, fish, and small mammals.

DID YOU KNOW?

- By coincidence, the two main fossil specimens of *Compsognathus* had their tail broken in exactly the same place.

- Many scientists think the feathers kept the animal warm at night. It may also have made *Compsognathus* more attractive to potential mates.

- The eyes were huge. They almost certainly gave the dinosaur excellent eyesight and may have helped it to hunt at night.

Kentrosaurus

This dinosaur roamed Africa around 150 million years ago, chomping on plant after plant. What *Kentrosaurus* lacked in speed and agility it made up for with vicious spikes along its back, which were probably arranged in two upright rows. These could inflict terrible wounds on its enemies and warn other animals off attacking.

WHERE DID THEY LIVE?

The only remains are in Tanzania, East Africa, in the area of Tendaguru.

Africa

Tanzania

FACTS

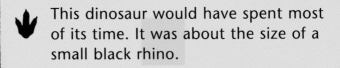

SIZE

- *Kentrosaurus* means "spiked lizard."

- Long hind legs suggest it was able to rear up to reach leaves.

- Lived during the Late Jurassic period.

Spines

The bony back plates grew longer and spikier toward the tail.

Head

Kentrosaurus had a tiny skull and an even tinier brain.

DID YOU KNOW?

Kentrosaurus had small, weak teeth, so experts think it swallowed stones to grind up plant food in its stomach— just like crocodiles today.

Its low front legs allowed *Kentrosaurus* to bend low to reach plants on the ground. Plant matter was scooped up in its toothless beak.

This dinosaur would have spent most of its time. It was about the size of a small black rhino.

Ornitholestes

Ornitholestes was a nimble predator that sprinted after prey. It was a small predator at a time when huge therapods ruled, so *Ornitholestes* was always watching out for danger with its large eyes. It was equipped with a balancing tail that helped it to run quickly. *Ornitholestes* probably preyed on small mammals, lizards, or unattended baby dinosaurs.

WHERE DID THEY LIVE?

Ornitholestes fossils have been found in Wyoming and Utah, USA.

Wyoming

Utah   USA

Teeth

The sharp upper and lower teeth fitted together like sharp bars to trap prey.

Thumb

The third finger acted like a thumb, allowing it to grip its victims.

FACTS

SIZE

- *Ornitholestes* means "bird robber" because it was thought to eat birds.

- It ate lizards, small mammals, and carrion.

- Lived during the Late Jurassic period.

DID YOU KNOW?

🐾 Its stiff tail worked as a stabilizer and a rudder. The tail allowed it to make quick turns when chasing a victim.

🐾 A broken nose bone in the fossil's skull led many scientists to believe incorrectly that *Ornitholestes* had a crest on its snout.

🐾 The lightweight frame and slim, muscular legs made *Ornitholestes* quick and agile.

Ophthalmosaurus

Ophthalmosaurus was not a dinosaur but an ichthyosaur, a prehistoric swimming reptile. It swam the warm Jurassic seas, probably in search of fish and shelled squid. Its most notable feature was its huge eyes. The larger the eye, the better it was able to see in the murky depths of the ocean.

WHERE DID THEY LIVE?

Remains have been found in northern Europe and North and South America.

North America

Europe

South America

Eyes

Enormous eyes let in more light, allowing it to hunt for prey in dim waters.

Teeth

The long jaws were packed full of teeth for grasping wriggling prey.

FACTS

SIZE

- *Ophthalmosaurus* means "eye lizard."

- Intact fossil remains show it gave birth to live young underwater.

- Lived during the Late Jurassic period.

DID YOU KNOW?

The tail was deep and curved. It beat from side to side to move the animal along at high speed.

When ichthyosaur fossils were first discovered in England in the early eighteenth century, people thought they were the remains of extinct dolphins or crocodiles wiped out in the flood of Noah's Ark.

All four limbs were modified to form paddles for tight steering and quick "braking."

Seismosaurus

Seismosaurus was 105 ft (32 m) long. More than half of its length was made up by its tail. The tail had to be long to counterbalance its huge, heavy neck when it walked. Despite its size, *Seismosaurus* was a peaceful plant-eater. Food was swallowed without chewing and was digested in the enormous gut probably with the help of gastroliths—stones swallowed to help grind down food.

WHERE DID THEY LIVE?

The only remains have been discovered in New Mexico, USA.

USA

New Mexico

Teeth

The teeth were probably like long pegs used for raking pine needles from branches.

Neck

The neck was held at a slight upward angle from the ground.

FACTS

SIZE

- *Seismosaurus* means "earthshaker lizard."

- Food was swallowed without chewing and was digested in the gut.

- Lived during the Late Jurassic period.

DID YOU KNOW?

- Some scientists think that *Seismosaurus* would have found it difficult to lift its head higher than its shoulders.

- The tail was extremely long. It was made of about 80 small bones. It was very flexible and might have been flung like a whip. It would also have been used to support the body.

- The pillarlike legs ended in huge feet. These were ideal for spreading the dinosaur's immense weight.

Stegosaurus

This plant-eater had a secret weapon when it came to fending off enemies—a swishing tail armed with strong spikes. With a body the size of a truck, *Stegosaurus* was the largest of all the stegosaurs, a group of dinosaurs that lived for 70 million years. The plates running along the back of *Stegosaurus* may have helped to keep its temperature stable.

WHERE DID THEY LIVE?

Fossils are found in western USA and Portugal.

USA   Portugal

Back Plates

Bony plates ran along its back from head to tail. Scientists are still unsure what they were for.

FACTS

- *Stegosaurus* means "roofed lizard."

- Estimated to be around 30 ft (9 m) long.

- Lived during the Late Jurassic period.

SIZE

Tail

Two pairs of pointed spikes were used as a lethal weapon.

DID YOU KNOW?

At 1 in (2.5 cm) long, the brain probably weighed no more than one-thousandth of the animal's total body weight.

At first, the back plates were thought to overlap like roof tiles. Now they are known to have stood vertically (upright). They probably would not have offered the dinosaur much protection.

The head was tiny in relation to the body. The sloping shape of the back suggests that the head was kept low most of the time.

Acrocanthosaurus

Acrocanthosaurus was one of the biggest meat-eaters of the Early Cretaceous period. It could even have tackled gigantic plant-eaters. Its huge, sharp teeth and long claws made it a swift and ruthless killer. Footprints discovered in the USA show that it sped up to its prey and then lunged at its victim, slashing it to death with its teeth.

WHERE DID THEY LIVE?

Mainly in the southern U.S. states of Oklahoma and Texas, with some possibly east in Maryland.

USA

Spines

Spines on the back may have been used for self-defense.

FACTS

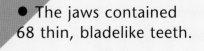

SIZE

- *Acrocanthosaurus* means "high spine."

- The jaws contained 68 thin, bladelike teeth.

- Lived during the Early Cretaceous period.

Claws

Vicious, hooked claws could rip at the flesh of prey and grip animals firmly.

DID YOU KNOW?

Acrocanthosaurus had a highly developed sense of smell. It would have been able to track its victims by scent.

The large eyes would have been able to spot prey at a distance. Above the eyes were hard "eyebrow bumps." These probably gave some protection from the claws of other killers.

The long, heavy tail balanced the animal's center of gravity over the hips. This kept it stable even when it was fighting.

Amargasaurus

One of the strangest dinosaurs ever discovered, *Amargasaurus* had a mane of bony spikes all the way down its neck and back. The double row of neck spikes would have made this dinosaur a hard target for hungry predators. Some experts think that the spikes on its back may have been covered with skin. This might have made an impressive display sail.

WHERE DID THEY LIVE?

The only remains are from the La Amarga canyon in Patagonia, west of Argentina.

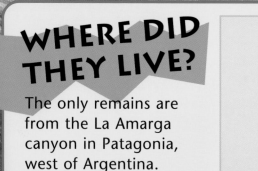

South America

Argentina

Spines

These long spines may have been strengthened by a horny covering.

FACTS

SIZE

- *Amargasaurus* means "lizard from La Amarga."

- The tallest neck spines were up to 20 in (50 cm) long.

- Lived during the Early Cretaceous period.

Tail

Held out straight, the long tail would have counterbalanced the long neck.

DID YOU KNOW?

Amargasaurus had a small head. Its nostrils were right at the top of the skull, above its eyes.

This dinosaur was surprisingly light for its size. This was because its vertebrae (backbones) were partly hollow. This means it weighed less than if they had been made of solid bone.

The animal was probably not very agile because of its size. The long spines would have restricted the movement of its neck.

Giganotosaurus

Giganotosaurus was the largest meat-eating dinosaur that ever hunted on land. With its jagged teeth it could bite through flesh like a knife slicing through butter. Its jaws were large enough to swallow an adult human whole! As if its size didn't make it terrifing enough, *Giganotosaurus* may have hunted in packs so it could bring down enormous plant-eating dinosaurs.

WHERE DID THEY LIVE?

Fossils have only been found in Argentina, but it possibly lived across South America.

South America

Argentina

Eyes

Ridges around its eyes obscured its forward vision.

FACTS

- *Giganotosaurus* means "giant lizard of the south."

- Its body was 46 ft (14 m) long.

- Lived during the Early Cretaceous period.

SIZE

Teeth

These were slender, like daggers. Serrated edges made them ideal for carving through flesh.

DID YOU KNOW?

Large nostrils and a well-developed sense of smell helped it to find living prey and dinosaur carcasses.

The first specimen of *Giganotosaurus* was discovered only in 1993 by an amateur fossil hunter in Argentina. About 70 percent of the skeleton has been preserved.

Although small in comparison with the body as a whole, its arms had strong hands with large claws.

Hypsilophodon

Not all plant-eating dinosaurs were big and slow. *Hypsilophodon* was so small and athletic that it could outrun most of its enemies. More than 20 skeletons were found close together on the Isle of Wight in England. This suggests that these animals lived in herds. It is not known how they died, but they may have been killed by a flood or drowned in quicksand.

WHERE DID THEY LIVE?

Fossils have been found on the Isle of Wight in England and in Portugal.

England
Isle of Wight
Europe
Portugal

Eyes

Large eyes meant it would have seen well in the gloom of dusk and dawn.

Legs

Long shins and short, powerful thighs made *Hypsilophodon* a swift runner.

FACTS

- *Hypsilophodon* means "high-ridged tooth."

- A small, lightweight body allowed it to sprint away from trouble.

- Lived during the Early Cretaceous period.

SIZE

DID YOU KNOW?

Chisel-like teeth lined the back of its jaws. It was one of the few dinosaurs of the time to chew its food.

When *Hypsilophodon* was first discovered, experts mistakenly thought it was a young *Iguanodon*. It was only 20 years later that scientist Thomas Huxley realized it was a new dinosaur.

Five-fingered hands would have supported its weight when it leaned forward to feed from the ground.

Baryonyx

The chance find of a huge claw led to one of the greatest dinosaur discoveries of the twentieth century—the fossil of a weird, meat-eating dinosaur. Its mighty thumb-claws earned *Baryonyx* the nickname "claws" when its remains were found in 1983. It was probably a top-class catcher of fish. Half-digested fossil scales of ancient fish were found close to the remains.

WHERE DID THEY LIVE?

Fossils have been discovered in England and Portugal.

England

Europe

Portugal

Hooked Thumb

A huge claw on the first finger of each hand probably served as a fishing tool and as a weapon.

Teeth

The sharp conical teeth were ideal for catching slippery prey.

FACTS

SIZE

- *Baryonyx* means "heavy claw."

- A long slender jaw bone made an S-bend like a crocodile's.

- Lived during the Early Cretaceous period.

DID YOU KNOW?

The long, strong arms suggest that *Baryonyx* may have been ableto walk on all fours.

The skull and long, flat jaw are like a crocodile's. The skull had twice as many teeth as many of its relatives. There were 64 in the lower jaw and 32 larger ones in the upper jaw.

Baryonyx might have been a warm-blooded dinosaur.

Deinonychus

Deinonychus had rows of saw-edged teeth and curved claws. This killer dinosaur was one of the most dangerous hunters of its time. Some scientists think it hunted in packs to track and attack prey that was much bigger than itself. It was a clever predator with a large brain for its size. It could inflict horrific wounds on its victims.

WHERE DID THEY LIVE?

Fossils have been found in the USA in Montana, Oklahoma, Wyoming, and Utah.

USA

Jaws

The teeth often broke off during an attack, but new ones grew in their place.

Sickle Claw

This was hinged like a switchblade. It had a bony core with a horny covering.

FACTS

- *Deinonychus* means "terrible claw."

- The sickle claw was like a 5 in (13 cm) blade used to attack victims.

- Lived during the Early Cretaceous period.

SIZE

DID YOU KNOW?

🐾 *Deinonychus* is thought to have been able to run quickly on its thin legs. It might have sprinted at 25 mph (40 km/h).

🐾 *Deinonychus* remains were discovered in 1964 by fossil expert John Ostrom. The large skull and muscular legs proved that the creature was a clever, agile killer.

🐾 Evidence suggests that *Deinonychus* had feathers on its body.

Iguanodon

Many meat-eating dinosaurs would have liked to make a meal of *Iguanodon*. But with huge thumb spikes to defend itself, this big plant-eater was not easy to beat. This highly successful dinosaur had a bony beak to clip off shoots, a special set of grinding teeth, and a long gut to help digestion. It was the first animal of its size to have such advanced eating equipment.

WHERE DID THEY LIVE?

Fossils have been found in England, Belgium, Germany, northern Africa, and western USA.

North America

Europe

North Africa

Beak

The sharp, toothless beak was used for nipping off twigs and leaves.

Hands

Five-fingered hands doubled as forefeet when the beast walked on all fours.

FACTS

- *Iguanodon* means "iguana tooth."

- The thumb spike ranged in size from 2 to 6 in (5–15 cm).

- Lived during the Early Cretaceous period.

SIZE

DID YOU KNOW?

The thumb spike may have been used for defense. It may also have been used for gathering leaves and shoots.

There were no teeth in the front of the snout where food was shoveled into a bony beak. However, there were rows of broad teeth in the back of the jaw to break food down.

The fifth or little finger could move like a thumb. It was able to grasp small items.

Kronosaurus

The ancient seas swarmed with huge reptiles snapping at anything that moved. One of the scariest was the mighty *Kronosaurus*. This huge reptile terrorized the oceans. Its massive skull had big jaws packed with terrifying teeth. These were weapons for butchering large reptiles and fish. It probably fed on fish, including sharks, squid, and other reptiles.

WHERE DID THEY LIVE?

Kronosaurus swam the shallow inland seas that covered Australia and Colombia.

Columbia

South America

Australia

Teeth

Up to 9 in (23 cm) long. Once in their grip, a victim had little chance of escape.

Flippers

Four paddlelike flippers propelled the animal through the water at great speed.

FACTS

SIZE

- *Kronosaurus* means "Titan lizard."

- It was 23–30 ft (7–9 m) long.

- Lived during the Early Cretaceous period.

DID YOU KNOW?

Fossil remains tell us what it looked like, but it is unknown whether it laid eggs on land or had live births at sea.

The best known *Kronosaurus* skeleton is at Harvard University in the USA. It is jokingly called Plasterosaurus. This is because of the amount of plaster of Paris used in its reconstruction.

The huge head was up to a third of the length of the body. The jaws were packed with muscles for crushing animal bones and shells.

Ouranosaurus

This big, heavy, plant-eating dinosaur had powerful jaws. They were perfect for tearing off and grinding up leaves. Fossil remains show that *Ouranosaurus* had extra-long spinal bones on its back. Some experts think that the bones supported a tall sail that the reptile used to maintain a comfortable temperature.

WHERE DID THEY LIVE?

Niger

Africa

Found in Niger, Africa, at a time when the region was almost as hot as it is today.

FACTS

- *Ouranosaurus* means "monitor lizard."

- Its sail made it look bigger and may have put off predators.

- Lived during the Early Cretaceous period.

SIZE

Spine

The long spine bones may have supported a "sail" to warm and cool the beast's blood.

Tail

This helped balance if the animal reared up to feed on leaves high up in the trees.

DID YOU KNOW?

Thumb spikes made effective weapons. The smallest of the other four fingers was mobile enough to help gather food.

Ouranosaurus lived before modern flowering plants appeared. It probably fed on plants such as horsetails, ginkgoes, cycads, ferns, and young conifers.

The skull has a pair of bumps on the nose. These have no obvious function. It may be that only males had them.

Psittacosaurus

This scary-looking but harmless animal once lived in great numbers all over eastern Asia. *Psittacosaurus* had a sharp, parrotlike beak that it used to strip leaves off trees. It would only have been waist high against a human so it had long arms to pull down branches. It needed to eat a lot to get enough energy. It may have gathered in herds to fight against attackers.

WHERE DID THEY LIVE?

Found in Mongolia, Russia, China, and Thailand.

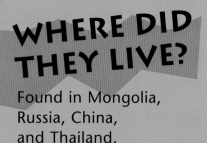

Russia

Mongolia

China

Thailand

FACTS

- *Psittacosaurus* means "parrot lizard."

- There are more than 400 specimens of *Psittacosaurus*.

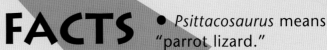

SIZE

- Lived during the Early Cretaceous period.

Beak

This was made from bone. At its tip was a rostral bone, a feature unique to horned dinosaurs.

DID YOU KNOW?

Some experts believe that *Psittacosaurus* relied on camouflage to hide from hungry killer dinosaurs.

The first *Psittacosaurus* fossil was found in 1922, on the American Museum of Natural History's third expedition to Mongolia. It was named the next year by U.S. expert Henry Fairfield Osborn.

Some *Psittacosaurus* fossils contain smoothly polished pebbles. It swallowed stones to help with digestion.

Arms

These were long enough to use to pass food to its mouth.

Pterodaustro

Pterodaustro was one of the oddest of all flying reptiles. It had long, upturned jaws lined with up to 500 thin, bendy teeth. These filtered food from the water. *Pterodaustro* once patrolled the skies of South America while huge dinosaurs roamed the land beneath. Its wings were made of tough, leathery skin supported by the animal's long fourth fingers.

WHERE DID THEY LIVE?

Only known to San Luis Province in Argentina.

South America

Argentina

Jaws

The jaws were lined with hundreds of narrow teeth.

FACTS

SIZE

- *Pterodaustro* means "wing of the south."

- The teeth were used to filter tiny plants and animals from the water.

- Lived during the Early Cretaceous period.

DID YOU KNOW?

Because of its filter habit, it is often called the flamingo pterosaur. Some artists have even drawn it in pink.

Pterodaustro had well-developed eyesight but a poor sense of smell. Good vision was more useful for detecting plankton swarms in the waters far below.

Its long, prominent lower teeth were paired with small teeth in its upper jaw.

Wings

The wings were made of skin strengthened with tough fibers.

Suchomimus

Around 100 million years ago, a killer dinosaur terrorized the waters of Africa. *Suchomimus* probably waded into the water on its two legs and caught giant fish on the massive claws on its thumbs. It may also have hidden in the rushes, waiting for a dinosaur to bend down to drink. In a single lunge, its jaws could have crunched its victim's flesh and bones.

WHERE DID THEY LIVE?

Niger

Africa

The only known fossil was found in 1997, near the Tenere Desert of Niger, West Africa.

Spines

Tail spines along the backbone may have supported a fleshy fin.

Teeth

These locked together, creating a narrow mesh from which fish could not escape.

FACTS

SIZE

- *Suchomimus* means "crocodile mimic."

- *Suchomimus* had about 100 teeth, which were not serrated.

- Lived during the Early Cretaceous period.

DID YOU KNOW?

Nostrils sat on top of the snout like a crocodile's. This allowed the killer to lie hidden in the water.

The sail on its back may have been brightly colored for use in mating displays.

The sail may also have soaked up the sun's early-morning rays so that it warmed up quickly.

Carcharodontosaurus

Carcharodontosaurus was one of the scariest carnivores ever to roam the planet. A predator as large as this one needed plenty of meat. This huge dinosaur had sharp jagged teeth that could easily slice through its victim's flesh. It was larger than three family-sized cars and weighed more than a hundred fully grown people. Its immense size gave it a big advantage against other dinosaurs.

WHERE DID THEY LIVE?

Fossils have been found in Morocco and Niger.

Morocco

Niger

Africa

Teeth

Its long, jagged teeth were serrated like steak knives.

FACTS

SIZE

- *Carcharodontosaurus* means "shark-toothed lizard."

- Estimated to be 44 ft (13.5 m) long.

- Lived during the Mid-Cretaceous period.

Claws

Fearsome claws designed for tearing flesh were located on the hands and feet.

DID YOU KNOW?

Its thick, heavy tail looked as though it could kill or seriously injure its enemies with a powerful blow.

Its skull shows that this huge creature's brain was only half as big as *T.rex*'s and about one-eighth the size of a human brain. The beaklike shape of its skull may have been useful for reaching into rotting carcasses.

Its jaws were huge and it had teeth that were up to 8 in (20 cm) long.

Spinosaurus

One of the biggest of all meat-eating dinosaurs, *Spinosaurus* was a powerful predator. It tore at its victims with massive, crocodilelike jaws and rows of sharp teeth. It mainly fed on fish. It had tall spines on its back. These were probably covered with skin, giving it a sail. It probably lived along a shoreline and shared swamps with other predators.

WHERE DID THEY LIVE?

Fossils have been found in the Western desert of Egypt, and in Morocco.

Morocco

Egypt

Africa

Teeth

Its long teeth were rounded and peglike, similar to a crocodile's.

Spine

Bladelike spines extended from the dinosaur's strong backbone.

FACTS

- *Spinosaurus* means "spine lizard."

- No complete fossils of the skull exist.

- Lived during the Mid-Cretaceous period.

SIZE

DID YOU KNOW?

- The spines of the dinosaur's backbone were up to 11 times as tall as the vertebrae from which they grew.

- The skull is one of the longest known in a carnivorous (meat-eating) dinosaur. It may have been 5ft 9 in (1.75 m) long, with a slender snout.

- The arms of *Spinosaurus* were much longer than those of most other large theropods. The creature may sometimes have walked on all fours.

Deinosuchus

Deinosuchus was a massive-jawed crocodile that was the largest ever known to stalk the wetlands of the world. This gigantic prehistoric killing machine lurked in lush swamps and marshes in North America more than 65 million years ago. With jaws that were as long as a man's body, it could easily have tackled dinosaurs weighing several tons.

WHERE DID THEY LIVE?

Found in various U.S. states from Texas to New Jersey, and across the border of Mexico.

USA

Legs

These were short and powerfully built to thrust the animal forward when attacking.

Jaws

The jaws were very strong and the teeth were suited to gripping, not biting.

FACTS

- *Deinosuchus* means "terrible crocodile."
- The largest of the prehistoric crocodiles.
- Lived during the Late Cretaceous period.

SIZE

DID YOU KNOW?

Deinosuchus wasn't just very long, it was also stout, with a heavy head and a reinforced neck.

Deinosuchus swallowed stones to use in its gizzard (a specialized stomach) for crushing and breaking bones from larger prey.

Counting their growth rings like the rings of a tree, experts think it took 35 years to reach adult size.

Edmontonia

Built like a tank, with a massive gut for breaking down large amounts of food, *Edmontonia* must have moved very slowly. It had little to fear from predators because its size and impressive body armor were enough to put off most attackers. An armor of studs and spikes meant tearing a chunk off it could result in snapping a tooth or being spiked.

WHERE DID THEY LIVE?

Edmonton, Alberta, in Canada, and in Montana, South Dakota, and Texas in the USA.

North America

FACTS

- *Edmontonia* means "of Edmonton," where the first fossils were found.

- Spikes protected its neck and flanks from predators' side attacks.

SIZE

- Lived during the Late Cretaceous period.

Armor

Its back was covered in bony plates, studs, and spikes.

Beak

The front of the jaws formed a toothless, horn-covered beak.

DID YOU KNOW?

Edmontonia had a short neck and short legs. These were ideal for feeding on ferns, cycads, and other low-lying plants.

So many fossils of *Edmontonia* have been found that it has been quite easy for experts to reconstruct the whole dinosaur. It likely lived in the woodlands of prehistoric North America.

Massive slabs of bone covered the skull for extra protection. These made a natural "crash helmet."

Gallimimus

Gallimimus was an Olympic sprinter of a dinosaur. Not many predators could have caught the birdlike beast as it sped along. It was half bird and half lizard, with a long, stiff tail, legs like an ostrich, and a toothless beak. It snapped up small creatures such as lizards, and perhaps even the buried eggs of other dinosaurs.

WHERE DID THEY LIVE?

Fossils have been found in the Bayshin Tsav region of southeastern Mongolia.

Mongolia

Asia

Hands

The hands ended in three long, flexible fingers tipped with small claws that could grip.

Eyes

Eyes on the side of its head suggest that *Gallimimus* would have had an all-round view.

FACTS

SIZE

- *Gallimimus* means "bird mimic."

- It was a fast runner and could possibly reach 43 mph (70 km/h).

- Lived during the Late Cretaceous period.

DID YOU KNOW?

Gallimimus walked upright on powerful back legs. If alarmed, the dinosaur could reach fast speeds over short distances.

Although it wasn't very well-known before, *Gallimimus* became famous in 1993 when a herd of them were featured in the movie *Jurassic Park*.

It may have eaten small insects, leaves, and berries, and possibly dinosaur eggs scooped from the ground with its claws or long, shovel-like bill.

Pteranodon

One of the largest of all the flying reptiles discovered so far, *Pteranodon* soared across the North American skies looking like a cross between a giant bat and a large pelican. Its wings were as wide as a small aircraft and yet it weighed no more than a large turkey. It probably lived in clifftop colonies, where it could launch itself to look for food.

WHERE DID THEY LIVE?

Found in central USA, in Kansas, Alabama, Nebraska, Wyoming, and South Dakota.

USA

Wings

Each thin wing was held up by the front limb and long fourth finger.

Beak

It may have had a large, drooping pouch below its beak to store fish in.

FACTS

SIZE

- *Pteranodon* means "winged and toothless."

- *Pteranodon* was not a dinosaur, but it was a pterosaur.

- Lived during the Late Cretaceous period.

DID YOU KNOW?

🐾 Like the wings of a bat, the wings of *Pteranodon* were made from light, flexible, and strong skin.

🐾 Some experts think *Pteranodon* had oily, featherlike hair to keep it warm and dry. No one really knows because any fur would have rotted away long before the animal's bones started to fossilize.

🐾 Its long crest may have balanced its heavy bill as *Pteranodon* scooped fish from the sea. It may also have helped with steering while it was flying.

Quetzalcoatlus

Quetzalcoatlus may have been the largest creature ever to take to the air. This incredible flying reptile could have stayed in the air for hours as it scanned the surface of rivers and lakes for fish to scoop up in its massive, toothless beak. Its wings would only have been attached to the top of its legs, so it may have walked upright with its wings folded.

WHERE DID THEY LIVE?

First discovered in Big Bend National Park, Texas, USA, and then in Alberta, Canada.

North America

Eyes

Large eyes meant it could spot prey from high in the air.

Beak

A long beak with sharp edges was ideal for snapping up slippery fish.

FACTS

- *Quetzalcoatlus* means "plumed serpent."

- The bones of flying reptiles were hollow, for lightness.

- Lived during the Late Cretaceous period.

SIZE

DID YOU KNOW?

- Its nostrils were high on its head so that they didn't fill with water when it plunged its beak into a river or lake.

- So far, more than 100 species of prehistoric flying reptiles have been discovered. They range in size from *Quetzalcoatlus* down to *Sordes*, which was about the size of a pigeon.

- A light but strong layer of skin would have covered the bones of each wing.

Saltasaurus

Saltasaurus lived in South America about 75 million years ago. It was a member of a group of giant, long-necked dinosaurs called sauropods. They walked slowly, carefully and quietly, like elephants. *Saltasaurus* had a long, sturdy tail that supported its weight as the leaf-eater reared up to feed on foliage high in the trees.

WHERE DID THEY LIVE?

Found in northwest Argentina in South America, in the area around Salta Province.

South America

Argentina

Teeth

Peglike teeth stripped leaves off branches.

FACTS

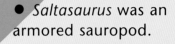

SIZE

- *Saltasaurus* means "Salta lizard."
- *Saltasaurus* was an armored sauropod.
- Lived during the Late Cretaceous period.

Armor

Well protected by its armor, which covered its back, tail, and neck.

DID YOU KNOW?

- Like many plant-eating dinosaurs, *Saltasaurus* had a very large body, a small head, and a long neck. This meant it could stretch up to reach leaves or fruits on high branches.

- *Saltasaurus* was a very big dinosaur, but eggs of its close relatives found in 1997 in Patagonia, Argentina, were only around 4 in (10 cm) long.

- Some scientists believe that sauropods used their long tails as weapons, to inflict stinging blows on their enemies.

Tyrannosaurus

Tyrannosaurus was one of the largest and most terrifying creatures the world has known. It once lived in what is now North America. It was so strong that it would have been able to overpower almost any other animal around at the time. Its huge jaws were filled with daggerlike teeth that could rip prey apart with one or two bites.

WHERE DID THEY LIVE?

Found throughout western North America.

North America

Teeth

The huge teeth would have sliced skin and crunched bone easily.

FACTS

- *Tyrannosaurus* means "tyrant lizard."

- *Tyrannosaurus* has a small brain for such a big animal.

- Lived during the Late Cretaceous period.

SIZE

DID YOU KNOW?

The skin of *Tyrannosaurus* was almost certainly covered in scales, like those on crocodiles.

Tyrannosaurus young probably had feathers, but adult *Tyrannosaurus* didn't need feathers to control their body heat.

Tyrannosaurus had bigger teeth than any other carnivorous dinosaur. The teeth in the upper jaw were larger than most of the teeth in the lower jaw. The largest was 13 in (33 cm).

Arms

Experts disagree on the use of these two-fingered hands and tiny but powerful arms.

Triceratops

With a mighty, helmetlike head with horns, and weighing as much as a small automobile, *Triceratops* was a giant among dinosaurs. Few predators would have dared to pick a fight with it. On some adults, the eye-horns grew to more than 3 ft (0.9 m) in length. *Triceratops* would have used these lethal weapons to fend off meat-eaters.

WHERE DID THEY LIVE?

Colorado, Wyoming, Montana, South Dakota in the USA. Alberta and Saskatchewan, Canada.

North America

Teeth

Up to 40 columns of teeth grew on each side of its jaw.

FACTS

- *Triceratops* means "three-horned face."

- Males possibly had larger skulls and horns than females.

- Lived during the Late Cretaceous period.

SIZE

Horns

Three sharp horns might have been used to scare off predators.

DID YOU KNOW?

Most dinosaurs are known from just a few specimens, but the fossil finds of *Triceratops* include hundreds of skulls.

With five teeth per column and 40 columns of each side of the jaw, *Triceratops* had 432 teeth in total. If any tooth was damaged or broken, another would grow in its place.

Triceratops had pillarlike legs, a bit like those of a rhino, to support its huge, bulky body.

Troödon

Troödon was rather small for a dinosaur. It stood no taller than an adult man. But scientists think that it could see better than any dinosaur, homing in on prey with deadly accuracy. It was able to run fast on its muscular back legs. It probably hunted down almost anything that it could tear apart with its sharp teeth, bony fingers, and clawed toes.

WHERE DID THEY LIVE?

Found in Montana, Alaska, and Wyoming in the USA, and in Alberta, Canada.

North America

Claws

The three long, bony fingers had sharp claws used for gripping prey.

Eyes

Big eyes let *Troödon* hunt in dim light or at night.

FACTS

SIZE

- *Troödon* means "wounding tooth."

- First discovered in 1855, it was one of the first dinosaurs found in North America.

- Lived during the Late Cretaceous period.

DID YOU KNOW?

The tail was long and muscled with a whippy tip. It could be swung quickly to help balance while *Troödon* ran.

Some experts believe *Troödon* was among the most intelligent dinosaurs. It had a large brain in relation to its body mass and had better vision than most other creatures of its kind.

Scientists now believe that *Troödon* was probably covered in feathers.

Velociraptor

Velociraptor may have stood only knee-high to its prey, but it made up for its small size with its ferocity. This small but very intelligent predator roamed the plains of what is now Mongolia, alongside other deadly meat-eating dinosaurs. It was one of the most advanced killers of its day. It had a big brain, so it was probably intelligent and alert.

WHERE DID THEY LIVE?

Found in Omnogovi and Tugrugeen Shireh in Mongolia, and in Chinese Inner Mongolia.

Mongolia
•
Asia

Jaws

Sharp and saw-edged, for slicing chunks of flesh from prey.

Claws

Sickle-shaped claws on each of its feet measured more than 2.5 in (6.5 cm).

FACTS

- *Velociraptor* means "speedy plunderer."

- Its head was large in relation to the body, but it was lightweight.

- Lived during the Late Cretaceous period.

SIZE

DID YOU KNOW?

Velociraptor had a very long tail, which could be almost twice the length of its body. It was stiffened by large bony projections on its backbone and bony tendons on the underside.

From the shape of its hip bones, some scientists think that *Velociraptor* may have sat upright like a dog, rather than crouching on its belly.

Scientists now believe that *Velociraptor* was probably covered in feathers.

Glossary

Agile/agility – moves quickly and easily

Avian – relating to birds, characteristic of birds

Camouflage – the surface coloring or patterning that helps an animal blend in with the plants, rocks, and soil

Carcass – the body of a dead animal

Carnivore – a meat-eater

Carrion – the rotting flesh of dead animals

Counterbalance – to balance one weight against another. Many dinosaurs had long, heavy tails to counterbalance the weight of their bodies.

Early Cretaceous – the geological period from around 145 million years ago to around 99 million years ago

Extinction – the disappearance of an entire species

Forelimb – the front part of a four-limbed animal: a foreleg, flipper, or wing

Fossil – the remains of a plant or animal from the very distant past

Gastroliths – small stones in the gut used to grind up tough plants

Herbivore – a plant-eater

Incisor – a front tooth for cutting food

Jurassic – the geological period from 199 million years ago to 145 million years ago

Limestone – a sedimentary rock

Mane – the long hair growing on the back of or around the neck of some animals

Mid-Triassic – the geological period from about 245 million years ago to about 228 million years ago

Nimble – quick and light in movement

Palate – the roof of the mouth

Permian – the geological period from about 299 million years ago to about 250 million years ago

Predator – an animal that hunts and kills other animals for food

Prey – an animal that is hunted by a predator

Pterosaur – an ancient flying reptile with skin-covered wings

Retractable – to draw or shrink back

Rostral bone – a bone that was located at the tip of the upper jaw

Sauropod – a type of large plant-eating dinosaur

Scavenger – a dinosaur or other animal that eats the dead remains of other creatures

Scute – a thin structure like a plate

Serrated – having an edge like a saw

Skeleton – the frame made of bone inside the bodies of humans and animals that protects the soft inner parts and to which the muscles are attached

Shale – a fine grain sedimentary rock. It is a mix of layers of minerals.

Specimen – an individual taken as an example of a species for examination

Stout – bulky in figure

Streamlined – ideally shaped for movement

Sturdy – strongly and solidly built

Tendon – a tough cord or band of dense white tissue that connects a muscle with another part of the body, such as a bone

Triassic – the geological period from about 250 million years ago to about 200 million years ago

Valve – a flaplike structure in an organ, such as the heart, that controls the one-way passage of fluid through that organ

Index

Picture Credits

Dreamstime: 8/9 Lindsay Douglas, 12/13 Tim Pleasant, 16/17, 70/71 Pancaketom, 20/21 Arievdwolde, 22/23 Lruet, 24/25 Mikhail Laptev, 26/27 Mopic, 28/29, 74/75 Myroslav Prylypko, 30/31 Anna Zhuk, 32/33, 80/81 Olga Khoroshunova, 34/35, 66/67, 68/69 Luis Carlos Jiminez, 36/37, 56/57, 92/93 Stryjek, 40/41 Vladimir Laroshenko, 44/45, 76/77 Grondin Franck Olivier, 46/47 Tramontana, 50/51 Nightbox, 54/55 Piccaya, 58/59 Watch The World, 64/65 Roman Zaremba, 72/73 Katrina Brown, 78/79 Rotislav Glinsky, 82/83 Roman Borodaev, 84/85 Mikhail Laptev, 86/87 Ammit, 88/89 Noamfein, 90/91 Propix, 94/95 JF123; **Shutterstock**: 10/11 Katerina Leigh, 14/15 Dimitry Pichugin, 18/19 Dirk R, 38/39 Glenn Nagel, 42/43 Keren Segev, 48/49 Dirk Ercken, 52/53 Photo Xite, 60/61 Marcel Mizik, 62/63 Goran Turina

All dinosaur artworks courtesy of **IMP**